SELLING
Rules!

SELLING
Rules!

52 ways you can achieve sales success

written by **MURRAY RAPHEL**
illustrated by **STEVE HICKNER**

BRIGANTINE MEDIA

Brigantine Media
211 North Avenue, St. Johnsbury, Vermont 05819
Phone: 802-751-8802 | Fax: 802-751-8804
Email: neil@brigantinemedia.com
Website: www.brigantinemedia.com

ISBN: 978-1-9384065-3-9

Dedication

To Sara and Harry, my mother and father.

They knew from the beginning.

My birth announcement appeared in the *Troy (NY) Record* and included an interview with my parents. The reporter asked my parents what they expected from me: "They have great plans for Murray's future. As a matter of fact they have set their minds on this point. No doctor or lawyer for them. Murray is destined to be a salesman."

The Rules

The Rules

Persevere.

TOM, THE TIE salesman, was an annual visitor to our clothing store.

We never bought anything from Tom because his ties were all made from polyester fabric. The ties we carried were made of natural fabrics: cotton, silk, wool.

One day when Tom appeared, I said, "Tom, you know we don't carry polyester ties. When are you going to stop coming to see us?"

He answered, "It depends on which one of us dies first."

McGraw-Hill did a survey on how many calls a salesperson had to make to a new prospect to achieve an initial sale.

The answer: four.

Many salespeople give up after the first try. Or second. Or third. Rejection is difficult to accept. And then a competitor appears on the scene and makes the sale because the first salesman did not persevere.

Internet advertising gives you new tools to persevere. You can remarket to prospects who visit your site. You can follow that potential customer all around the Internet with advertisements and messages. Those ads that appear are little reminders to the customer that you're still around.

You can also send an e-mail to a customer who does all-but-order in your shopping cart. Maybe the customer found the item elsewhere, or decided not to purchase it . . . but just maybe, she was distracted during the process and will buy the product from you when you let her know she didn't quite get the order finished.

Perseverance. The best salespeople have it in spades.

RULE
2

Listen.

A MAN WAS invited by a prominent hostess to all her parties because her guests told her how much they enjoyed his company. The hostess was confused. He was no life of the party. He was, in fact, quiet and subdued. Why did her guests like the man so much?

At her next party, the hostess introduced the man to one of her guests and then, unobtrusively, remained in close proximity to hear his technique. It was very simple. After being introduced he would ask the person he just met, "Tell me about yourself . . ." And then he would just . . . listen.

He listened to people talk about their jobs,

their family, their hopes, their dreams. Where would they like to go on their next vacation? Why? For how long?

Later, everyone told the hostess what a marvelous addition he was to the party.

Here's why: People who listen seem to care more about people. They come across as more open-minded and thoughtful. Those who continually talk come across as pompous and self-centered.

There are lots of ways to listen to your customers. Free or low-cost Internet survey tools such as Survey Monkey or Zoomerang make it easy to obtain customer feedback. Listening to your customers may be the best way to be sure that you are selling what your customers really want to buy.

Dale Carnegie, author of *How to Win Friends and Influence People*, said, "You can make more friends in two months by being interested in other people than you can in two years by trying to get other people interested in you."

Smile.

START EVERY SALES call or conversation with a smile.

A major telephone company had its operators call customers for new marketing services. Half the salespeople were told to smile while giving the selling message over the phone. Half were told not to smile.

A survey company then asked the customers if they knew if the salesperson was smiling when talking. More than 80 percent of the customers could discern if the salesperson was smiling simply by listening to them.

Smiling not only helps sell, it also has beneficial results for the employees themselves. Jessica Pryce-Jones, author of *Happiness at Work* and CEO of iOpener found that the happiest employees are 180 percent more energized than their less content colleagues and spend twice as much time on their work as unhappy workers. They also take 66 percent less sick leave than the unhappiest workers.

When you interview a job applicant, count the number of times he smiles. That's a good indication of how he'll do on the job.

When you fish, go where the fish are.

MOST COMPANIES SPEND five times as much money looking for new customers as they spend on current customers. That's a bad allocation of resources.

Try spending more on the customers you have. Your current customers know you, trust you, and (most importantly) spend money with you. It is far, far easier to sell more to your current customers than to find new ones.

Brian Wolff, author of several books on loyalty marketing, did a 1994 study in the supermarket industry that found that the top 30 percent of customers were responsible for 80 percent of revenues and all of the company's profits.

Wolff recommended that supermarkets (and other companies) reward their best customers by giving them special discounts. As Wolff's ideas spread throughout the industry, loyalty cards and data collection became ubiquitous. Supermarkets and other industries like hotels and airlines began rewarding loyal customers more than new customers. Today, Amazon keeps track of every purchase you make and encourages ever-increasing levels of loyalty through the many benefits in its "Prime" program.

In the early 1900s, Reverend Russell Conwell gave one speech more than 6,000 times, raising five million dollars to found Temple University. The title of the speech: "Acres of Diamonds."

Conwell's theme: "Your diamonds are not in far distant mountains or in yonder seas. They are in your own backyard if you but dig for them."

Dare to be different.

YEARS AGO, WE were planning our annual winter sale and looking for an idea to make us different from all the other stores running winter sales. I suggested having a sale for three hours on New Year's Day.

My colleagues were not enthusiastic. They said:

"All the other stores in town are closed so we won't get the usual traffic."

And: "It's the morning after New Year's Eve. People will still be sleeping."

And: "People stay home on New Year's Day guzzling beer and pretzels in front of the TV set watching the Bowl games. It's a tradition."

But we tried the sale anyway and created a new tradition.

We sent a mailing to our customers announcing a "private" winter sale from noon to 3:00 p.m. on New Year's Day. We said the announcement they were reading was sent only to those on our mailing list and would not be advertised in any other way.

We arrived an hour early to check the merchandising and signs. When we approached the store we saw lines of people standing outside.

Our first thought was there was a break-in, a fire, something . . .

No. The customers were waiting for the store to open.

We did more business in the three hours of our New Year's Day sale than we did any *week* of the year!

Surely the other stores in town would follow our lead and also capture this success.

Amazingly, they did not for ten years!

When asked why, they said, "No one goes shopping on New Year's Day. It's a tradition."

Know the "lifetime value"
of your customers.

I MET STEW Leonard at his famous supermarket in Norwalk, Connecticut, and he explained why each customer is important: "The lifetime value of a customer in a supermarket is about $246,000. Every time a customer comes through our front door I see, stamped on her forehead in big red letters, *$246,000!* I'm never going to make that person unhappy with me. I can't afford to lose a customer to my competition."

Stew told me the event that hammered home this philosophy.

When Stew's store first opened, a customer returned a quart of buttermilk she had bought at his store. She said it didn't "smell right."

Stew smelled the carton and told her, "Smells right to me." He called over his milk manager and the manager agreed that the buttermilk was fine.

The woman disagreed. Stew and the woman then argued back and forth over who was right. Finally, Stew gave the customer her money back.

The woman left. But not before she gave him this parting shot: "I don't like the way you treated me. I'm never shopping here again."

Stew realized he had done the right thing (he refunded the customer's money) but he had the wrong attitude. He lost $246,000 arguing over a quart of buttermilk.

There is a three-ton stone in front of Stew Leonard's flagship store. Engraved in the stone are these words:

Rule 1: The customer is always right!

Rule 2: If the customer is ever wrong, reread Rule 1.

Create a "want."

THE MAN WHO invented the vacuum cleaner went bankrupt.

He sold the patents to a Mr. Hoover who brought this new-fangled "electric broom" to department store buyers.

The buyers turned down the vacuum cleaner. Their reason: There was no need for this contraption. People bought inexpensive brooms to clean floors and rugs. Who would want to spend more money for an electrical gadget that did the same job?

So Hoover hired a sales force that went door to door. They walked into living rooms all over America, spilling dirt on rugs and then whisking them clean with this new "vacuum cleaner."

Soon, every home had to have one.

Soon, department stores quickly stocked vacuum cleaners because their customers wanted them.

What happened? A "want" was created by a clever marketing campaign.

And now vacuum cleaners are being challenged by a more sophisticated "want." Thanks to the invention of the robot vacuum, customers today want the appliance to do the cleaning by itself!

Today's successful salespeople are not need-fillers. They are want-creators.

As little children we are asked by adults, "What do you want to be when you grow up?" No one asks, "What do you need to be?" The reason is simple. If you "want" something strong enough you will produce it, work for it, or buy it.

Always think about "you."

THE WORD "YOU" is the one of the most important words in selling.

Advertising expert Paul Suggett rated the ten most important "power" words in advertising. Number one on his list was "you."

"You" keeps you reading. In the 1960s, the weekly news magazine *Newsweek* was struggling to compete with its larger rival, *Time*. *Newsweek* was able to gain readers partly because of its subscription letter written by copywriter Ed McLean and used for nearly 15 years. The letter returned a higher rate of subscriptions than all the other letters *Newsweek* tried. More than 100 million copies of this letter were mailed!

The letter began, "If the list upon which I found your name is any indication, this is not the first—nor will it be the last—subscription letter you receive. Quite frankly, your education and income set you apart from the general population and make you a highly rated prospect for everything from magazines to mutual funds . . ."

The word "you" is used 26 times on just the first page of the subscription letter!

AdEspresso, a Facebook advertising company, recently analyzed 37,259 Facebook ads and found out that the most popular word used was "you." (Other top contenders: "free," "now," "and "new.") It worked fifty years ago and it still works today—"you" is the magic word!

Be odd.

"The god delights in the odd number."
—*Virgil*

ODD PRICES SAY "bargain" to the customer. If a product sells for $29.99 it "sounds" less expensive than $30. In fact, it even "feels" closer to $20 than $30.

A test was given to women members of church groups and PTAs in middle income Chicago suburbs by Robert Schindler, assistant professor of marketing and behavioral science at the University of Chicago Graduate School of Business.

His team put together two booklets of clothing, furniture and shoe ads from out of town newspapers (so the women would not be prejudiced by names they knew).

They put even prices in one booklet and odd prices in another booklet for the same merchandise. Each group saw only ONE booklet. Here are the results:

- Odd prices had a positive effect.

- Reducing the item in price by as little as one cent increased the number of people who thought the advertised item was on sale, even though NONE of the ads said "sale."

A study did an analysis of final digit prices used by retailers. The number "9" was used 36 percent of the time.

The lure of odd pricing is the reason that Apple prices a laptop at $1,299.99, not $1,300. The one cent difference makes the consumer feel the laptop is in the $1,200 range and not the $1,300 range.

Odd.

But true.

Do what winners do.

EDWIN HOYT WENT to a men's clothing store to buy a jacket. When he went home that evening he was surprised to see that, in addition to purchasing the sport jacket, he had also bought additional merchandise: pants, shirts, and ties.

He wondered how that happened when he only planned to buy the jacket.

He returned to the store the next day. He told the salesman he was a writer. Would the salesman share with him the secret of selling him so much more than he planned to buy?

The salesman told Hoyt his selling methods. Hoyt became intrigued with the idea of finding out what techniques were used by top salespeople. For the next few years he traveled across the US asking top salespeople what made them successful. He discovered that almost all of them had the same ten characteristics. Here they are:

1 Work hard.

2 Be self-confident.

3 Have self-discipline.

4 Persevere.

5 Be flexible.

6 Have goals other than dollars.

7 Respect the buyer's good sense.

8 Learn from others.

9 Be able to handle big dollars.

10 Be a perfectionist.

Use Simple Selling Phrases

ELMER WHEELER WAS chosen as America's number one public speaker by a poll of 500 business clubs. He spoke to more than a million people in his lifetime. He had a unique ability to come up with just the right wording or phrase to sell merchandise.

He went to see King Gillette, owner of Gillette blades and said, "I have six words on this folded piece of paper. If you decide to use them, you pay my fee. If you don't, I leave." Gillette took the paper, unfolded it, read the words and wrote out a check. Here are the six words: "How are you fixed for blades?"

He was asked by representatives from America's drug stores to figure out how to increase sales at their lunch counters. He gave them the phrase that immediately put more money in the register. When

a customer asked for a malted milk shake, the clerk asked, "One egg or two?"

Wheeler was contacted by the salmon industry in the Northwest. Customers were used to opening a can of salmon and seeing the pink color. For some indescribable reason, a new salmon catch, when processed, turned white. Fearing the customer would not accept the product, the industry turned to Wheeler for help. He solved their anxiety and kept sales at a record pace by adding these words to the outside of the can: "This salmon guaranteed not to turn pink."

The Petroleum Institute asked Wheeler to come up with a phrase to have people buy more gas. Wheeler gave them three words that increased sales across the country. When someone pulled up to a station for gas, the attendants were instructed to simply ask this question: "Fill 'er up?"

Simple selling phrases make great slogans:

- IMAX theaters: Think big.

- Volkswagen: Think small.

- Walmart: Save Money. Live better.

- United Negro College Fund: A mind is a terrible thing to waste.

- Disneyland: The happiest place on earth.

- De Beers: A diamond is forever.

- Nike: Just do it.

Visualize your goal.

"Success or failure in business is caused more by mental attitude even than by mental capacities."
—*Walter Dill Scott, 1911*

THE SUCCESSFUL SALESPERSON acts with tremendous self-confidence. He is a strong believer in "imaging." He sees himself throwing the pass for the touchdown, setting a track record, and always making the sale.

His philosophy is this:

If I'm not making sales, it's not the weather, the economy, or the time of the year. It's me.

And if I *am* making sales, it's not the weather, the economy or the time of the year. It's me.

Somebody's buying something from somebody. How am I going to get them to buy from me?

The 1890 play, "A Pair of Spectacles," was adapted from the French by Sydney Grundy. The story is about a kind and gentle man who suddenly finds himself in all kinds of trouble. Here's why: When he left his home one morning, he picked up his miserly brother's eyeglasses. From that moment on, he became mean and distrustful.

The point: Look at life through the right glasses to understand, visualize, and achieve your goal.

Always give the customer a choice between something and something else.

HERE'S HOW IT works in a clothing store:

A man comes in to buy a shirt. You ask him which style he prefers ("Button down, spread collar, or tab collar?"). He chooses one.

You ask him which color ("Blue, yellow, beige?"). He chooses one. Now you say you have several ties that go well with the shirt he has chosen. Does he like a solid color tie, a stripe, or a print? He will choose one. You always give him a selection and then he makes a choice.

The sale continues. At no time is the customer asked if he wants to buy or not to buy. He is simply asked to make a choice between the selections offered.

This technique works for automobiles, wallpaper, insurance . . . any business. All you do is have a customer narrow the choices down to what he or she wants. At the same time, you confine the choices to what you want to sell.

Travel first class.

THE CHANGE HAPPENED to me years ago in a
New York hotel room. I had made a reservation for
their advertised room at a "special rate for buyers."

But the room was tiny, cramped, and overlooked
a ventilation shaft. One wall was mirrored to make
the room look larger.

"I want a bigger room that overlooks Central
Park," I said. "That's more expensive," said the bell-
hop. "This is the 'special rate' room."

I felt the "special" room was not special. I moved.
My new room was larger and I awoke in the morning

with a park panorama outside the window. My starting-the-day attitude was high. I felt good. Confident. First class.

Later, I thought about what happened and realized I was traveling through life as a second-class citizen. I was always searching for the lowest price instead of the highest quality.

Perhaps it was a throwback to childhood, scrunching up small in the train seat to pass as "under 12 years old" and entitled to the half-price children's rate.

Perhaps it was going out to dinner with my parents and knowing the never-said-but-understood commitment to order the least expensive item on the menu.

This early conditioning was part of my adult thinking.

But after experiencing the "special" hotel rate, I changed.

Here's why: Every good salesperson must have a healthy dose of self-confidence. It begins with what you think about yourself. Are you a second-class or first-class person?

You can't be a great salesman unless you think, act, and perform in a first-class manner.

Accentuate the positive.

DEPENDING ON THE product you sell, different words make a difference.

Don't end a presentation by telling the customer to "sign here." Ask the customer to "okay the paperwork" or "approve this form."

Don't say "price" or "cost." Say "investment."

Don't say "house." Say "home."

Don't say "sales pitch." Say "presentation."

Don't say "used car." Say "previously owned."

Don't say "pay." Say "save."

Don't say "down payment." Say "initial investment."

Don't say "contract." Say "agreement."

Don't say "buy." Say "own."

Don't use negative words like death, fail, lose, worry, or obligation.

Do use positive words like easy, guarantee, safety, comfort, or value.

The value of positive speaking was emphasized when the *Wall Street Journal* reported that 40 Republican congressmen received nine hours of language training and media coaching. The purpose of the program was to help lawmakers use words and phrases (tested in polling) to sell basic themes like education, social security, defense, and tax cuts.

Among the "power adjectives" they were told to use were "able" and "American" and avoid words like "inoperative," "cash flow," "feedback," and almost any word that ends in "ion."

As Bing Crosby crooned,

"You've got to accentuate the positive,
Eliminate the negative,
Latch on to the affirmative,
Don't mess with Mister In-Between."

Give your customers something extra.

*"What is least expected
is the more highly esteemed."*
—*Baltasar Gracián, Spanish Jesuit philosopher (mid 1600s)*

WHEN COMEDIAN AND entertainer Eddie Cantor was growing up in the 1920s on the lower East Side of New York City, he ran errands for housewives in his tenement building. In exchange for a piece of cake or a chunk of salami, he did their grocery shopping. But one thing puzzled him.

Why did all the housewives send him to the same store a distant ten blocks away? Why not shop a market that was closer? He offered to change to a nearer store to speed his delivery time but the housewives all said, "No."

The next time he went to the store to fill his orders, he watched carefully to see the reason. What he saw were mistakes! If an order was for a dozen rolls, the grocer put in thirteen.

Cantor pointed out the mistakes to the grocer. "No mistake," said the grocer. "It's good business to give something extra."

Years later, Cantor went back to see if he could find out if the grocer was still in business. The store was gone but he finally located the grocer. He was not on the East Side. He no longer worked in a store. He was chairman of the board of a chain of supermarkets.

RULE
17

Repeat.

A BASIC RULE of selling is to repeat the name of the product you're selling at least three times during your presentation.

Here's why: The audience may have missed seeing or hearing the name the first time. Direct marketers say the PS of a letter is the best-read part. The reader looks at the PS and says, "Hmmm, I wonder what they forgot to mention . . ."

The PS is a great place to repeat your main offer.

Give your customer different ways to buy your product. Offer ways for customers to buy directly on your website or let them click to a site where they can buy your products. And include your phone number. Too many websites neglect customers who want a human touch.

A leading shampoo manufacturer wanted to increase sales. The company analyzed its advertising and allocated more dollars for research, including focus groups in different cities.

And then, one day, a smart marketer suggested they simply add one word to the instructions for use of the company product.

They added the word. And sales increased 50 percent.

Here is the word: "Repeat."

Practice humility.

FEARGAL QUINN, WHOSE Superquinn super-markets were among the best in the world, gave a speech titled, "My Five Lessons in Humility." Here are the lessons:

First: "My customers know more than I do." Once you believe that, you must listen to customers and find out what they want. What customers want is often much different than what *you* think they want.

Second: "My employees know more than I do." Feargal listened to his employees and empowered them to make decisions so they could build a rapport with each customer.

Third: "Neither my employees nor I can be creative all the time." Feargal once attended a seminar where the speaker defined management as "getting results through other people." So Feargal learned to use customers to help him find exciting merchandising ideas (including new products).

Fourth: "What I knew yesterday is not enough for today." Change is happening all around us. Be ready and accepting of change, and be quick to adopt new ideas.

Fifth: "I'm not responding fast enough for my customer." Anticipate customers' needs and be quick to meet them.

Never give up.

"Whether you believe you can do a thing or not,
you are right."
—*Henry Ford*

TOO MANY SALESPEOPLE faced with a problem
shrug their shoulders and say, "It can't be done."

Wrong.

Think in terms of how it CAN be done. Ignore the
traditional excuses. Remember Winston Churchill's
speech he gave to the students at the Harrow School
in October 1941 in the middle of the constant bomb-
ing of England by the Germans.

Here it is:

"Never give up. Never. Never. Never. Never."

When you're on time, you're late.

I ALWAYS SET my watch five minutes ahead. When I look at my watch I just assume that's the correct time. That way when I make an appointment, I'm there before the specified time. If you're meeting with an executive to whom time is a precious commodity, he or she will appreciate your being there before the scheduled appointment.

F. G. "Buck" Rodgers, corporate vice president of marketing for IBM, called for a 9:00 a.m. sales staff meeting. At 9:30, people were still drifting in. At the end of the meeting he said, "Next week's meeting will start at nine a.m. exactly. Be on time."

At the next meeting, he looked at his watch. When it reached nine o'clock, he locked the door and began his briefing. For the next half hour there was knocking at the door as latecomers wanted to be admitted. Rodgers kept on talking, ignoring the interruptions.

When the meeting ended, he told the people who were there on time, "When you leave, the people who were not here on time will ask you what we talked about. You are not to tell them. If you do, you put your job in jeopardy. There's no reason someone who is late should benefit from you being on time."

The meeting broke up and as the participants left, those outside the room asked, "What happened?" "What did he talk about?" and were answered, "Sorry, I can't tell you."

The latecomers were shocked. Why couldn't their colleagues tell them what happened? Did it have something to do with their job? Were promotions discussed? Were new territories assigned? What?

At the following week's 9:00 a.m. meeting, everyone was seated by 8:45.

Sell good feelings
and solutions to problems.

THERE ARE ONLY two reasons that people buy what they buy.

What do you think they are? Needs and price? Nope.

Try this: Think of three recent ads you saw. Any three. OK, here are the questions:

1 How many items did you really need?

2 How many advertised the price?

Answers to both questions: None.

Our theory is that there are only two reasons people buy what you have to sell:

(a) Solutions to problems or

(b) Good feelings.

Solutions to problems: "Lose eight pounds in one month." "Increase your production ten percent in one year." "Reduce the time you spend shopping and cooking."

Good feelings: When a customer gets two dozen pictures of her child from the photography studio for the same price as one dozen. When you receive free two-day shipping for any order. When you buy a pair of shoes for yourself, a pair of shoes is donated to a child in need. What can you afford to give to your customers to make them feel better about their purchases?

Guarantee your work.

GUARANTEES WILL BRING you more business at very little cost. How about this one from retailer Lands End: "If you're not satisfied with any item, simply return it to us at any time for an exchange or refund of its purchase price. Guaranteed. Period."

That says it all.

Here's a shipping promise and guarantee from Nordstrom: "We'll ship almost anything on our site to anywhere in the United States—even Alaska, Hawaii and Puerto Rico—for free. No minimums. No kidding. Don't love it? Return it for free too. We mean it."

Hey, I want to do business with Nordstrom!

Cross pens are known for quality and craftsman-ship and their "lifetime guarantee." If one of their pens breaks, mail it back to Cross and they will send you a new pen.

How about this guarantee from the Hampton Inns? "Friendly service, clean rooms, comfortable surroundings, every time. If you're not satisfied, we don't expect you to pay. That's our commitment and your guarantee." That guarantee will make you sleep better!

Griot's Garage, a car care company, puts its life-time guarantee on its website (something you should do). "At Griot's Garage, we want you as a customer for life. Everything you purchase from us comes with a lifetime guarantee against defect. We want you to enjoy our quality product for 180 days and have fun with it! If you don't like it for any reason during this time, return it for a full refund or credit. After that, you're covered with our lifetime guarantee against defect, in which we will either repair it, replace it, or credit your purchase price if we are able to do neither."

Don't be concerned that customers will take advantage of your guarantee. Paul Foster, writing for "The Start Up Donut," says that less than one percent of customers will unfairly take advantage of your guarantee—and the profits from the new business you've gained by offering the guarantee will more than make up for any loss.

Under-promise and over-deliver.

WHEN VREST ORTON opened his Vermont Country Store in 1946 in the tiny village of Weston, Vermont (population 400), he did a good business with tourists. Wanting to expand, he decided to go into mail order. He called L. L. Bean in Freeport, Maine, who achieved success with his famous catalogue, and asked if he could come see him for advice. L. L. Bean agreed and Vrest went to Maine with several yellow pads and sharpened pencils for directions from the mail order pioneer.

"What do I have to do to be successful in mail order?" he asked Bean.

"Simple," said Bean, "just memorize one sentence and you can go home. Here it is: 'Make sure the story isn't better than the store.'"

What was L. L. Bean saying? This: whatever you tell the customer they will receive, make sure the product is even better than the description.

That's a recipe for happy customers.

Copy ideas from other businesses.

MY FRIEND RAY Considine and I proposed an Eleventh Commandment for business: "Thou Shalt Steal Every Idea Thou Can Find . . . and Make It Thine Own."

Yes, read the trade magazines for your industry. Google your competitors to see what they are up to. Look at similar stores when vacationing. Attend trade shows.

But also: steal ideas from marketers in different businesses.

If Amazon is offering two-day delivery for its best customers, can you afford to offer it to your best customers? Can you afford to *not* offer two-day delivery?

If some stores in town offer longer shopping hours and free gift-wrapping during the holiday season, maybe you should follow their lead.

When Southwest Airlines wanted to speed aircraft turnaround time, they did not observe other airlines. They went to the Indianapolis 500 to see how pit crews fuel and service racecars. This gave Southwest new ideas about equipment fitting, materials management, teamwork, and speed that enabled the airline to cut turnaround time in half.

Granite Rock wanted to improve the way it loaded gravel into trucks in its yards because its drivers had to leave trucks and fill out papers. The company watched automatic teller machines in banks. Now, drivers put a card in a machine because the loading process is automated.

New ideas for your business from are all around you—if you keep your eyes open and connect the dots.

Headline your benefits.

ADVERTISING GURU DAVID Ogilvy had his copywriters create as many as 100 headlines for the same ad, seeking just the right words to increase sales. He told his staff when they had written an effective headline, they had spent 70 percent of their clients' money.

Here's why: seven out of ten people read the headline of an ad. Only three out of ten keep on reading.

During my 40 years in retailing, I wrote at least 15,000 headlines. A handful of them worked every time we used them. Here is one of my favorites:

"Would You Buy a $50 Yves St. Laurent Shirt On Sale for $29?"

Substitute the original price, the name of the item, and the sale price for whatever you want to sell. This headline will always bring in customers—as long as the product's name is recognizable and the value is great.

Here's a fun headline that helped our business:

"The name is Mañana. But at $65 you'd better buy it today."

The product was a woman's jacket made in Mexico. We sold the entire stock of 48 pieces the same day the ad ran. We reordered and ran the exact same ad ten days later. And sold out again in 48 hours. We reordered again and sold out again.

Here are a few other successful headlines:

- Do You Make These Travel Mistakes?

- Here's How to Have a Long and Healthy Life

- How to Do Your Christmas Shopping in Five Minutes

If a headline works, repeat it. Some customers never saw it the first time. Other customers saw it and are reminded. And satisfied customers will tell others.

Use this "four-mula" for success.

THE IDEA ALWAYS works!

Make four phone calls a day to customers telling them about new merchandise just received you know they usually buy. Or about a special sale on their most liked items. Or any reason that gives them a personal benefit.

OR: Send four e-mails or text messages a day. One idea: Thank customers for their recent purchase from you.

OR: Give out four business cards a day. You meet new people every day. A waiter or waitress. A fellow Rotarian. The person next to you on the plane. Business cards are "miniature billboards." They tell who you are and what you do, and if you give enough away you're practicing the old Fuller Brush theory of knocking on enough doors and one will open.

OR: AFTO four times a day. Ask for the order. Too many salespeople present their case and wait for the customer to say "Okay, I'll buy it." Rarely happens. Ask for the order.

If you use only one of these techniques every day, that's more than 1,400 contacts a year. If only ten percent respond, you'll have more than 140 *extra* sales you would not have had.

Too lazy to write notes yourself? Now you can send a handwritten card from Bond.com, signed and sealed by a writing machine that can produce personalized notes. The machines have robotic arms that can hold a pen, a paintbrush, or a marker. You can use various handwriting styles, or have your own handwriting digitized. A new twist on an old idea!

Don't object to complaints.

WHEN SOMEONE COMPLAINS about a product they bought from you, the first thing to do is to listen. The same principles apply whether the complaint comes in person or online.

They've rehearsed what they're going to say, they expect negative feedback from you. They are ready to fight. So don't interrupt them. Listen.

When confronted with an in-person complaint, don't comment, don't look around, don't adopt the "I've heard all this before" exasperated look. Listen. And look at them while they're talking.

Then, when their conversation stops, wait a second, and carefully, softly say these ten words: "Tell me what you want and the answer is yes."

If the color in the shirt ran in the washing, if they were forced to go through a telephone drill of "Push 1 for . . . push 2 for . . ." and were not taken care of, if the book they ordered was not what they thought it would be—whatever the merchandise or complaint—simply say, "Tell me what you want and the answer is yes."

They can have a replacement of merchandise, their money back, money for gas for driving to your place of business—whatever they want. And make this offer with your apologies and thanks.

Here's what happens: the customer is at first confused, then bewildered, then amazed, and then, often, apologetic.

They are conditioned for confrontation. What they receive instead is kindness.

For an online complaint, the process is very similar. *Inc.* magazine recommends:

- Listening (taking every complaint seriously)

- Apologizing (if you've done something wrong)

- Solving the problem (reply privately with your offer)

- Thanking the customer

Solving complaints is one of the most important (and often one of the most neglected) parts of running a business.

Give away your merchandise.

WHEN FACED WITH a choice between reducing prices and giving away something free . . . give away something free.

Here's why: Your cost is less.

If you sell widgets for $50 each and put them on sale for $35, you reduce your profit by $15. Instead, keep the price the same but give your customer a gift/ supplement/auxiliary item that ties in with their purchase—free. If this free item has a retail value of $10, your cost is only $5 and you're ahead $10!

You'll make the customer happier because of the free gift.

We know a dry cleaner who never runs sales. But, every once in a while, to increase business, he "gives away" some dry cleaning. Bring in a suit to have cleaned and pressed and he'll clean and press another pair of pants . . . free. His actual cost of cleaning and pressing the extra pair of pants is far less than if he reduced the price of dry-cleaning the suit.

Figure it out. Add up the difference between the money you lose in a having a sale against what you lose in giving away something free.

The free item maintains a good profit. The sale item doesn't.

Don't worry if someone copies your best ideas.

IT'S TRUE. IMITATION *is* the sincerest form of flattery.

When someone asks, "Don't you worry someone will steal your idea?" your answer is, "But I've already done that one. I'm on to something new."

Many business people think their ideas are so special they must hide them from their competitors . . . and even their consultants.

That's why I consider most "non-disclosure" agreements a waste of time. An idea only becomes powerful when it is put into action. Somebody else has already thought of the idea, whether it's drones delivering packages or a smartphone app that helps you find the best restaurant on a road trip. It's making the idea a workable reality that is the hard part. The idea itself is worthless.

Rudyard Kipling wrote a poem about Sir Anthony Gloster, a self-made shipping tycoon. On his deathbed he relives his life to his son and refers contemptuously to his competitors, saying:

"They copied all they could follow, but they couldn't copy my mind,

And I left 'em sweating and stealing, a year and a half behind."

Choose success.

WHEN H. L. Hunt, the oil billionaire, was asked for the secret of success, he gave this four-step answer:

1   Decide what you want to do.

What are your personal goals as a salesperson? What do you want to sell? To whom? Where do you want to be a year from now? Five years from now?

2   Decide what you'll give up to do it.

You mean it's not a 40-hour-a-week job? (*That's right!*) You mean I have to constantly be aware of the competition and the customers and any changes they make? (*That's right!*) You mean I have to give up some of my hobbies or free time activities to concentrate more on selling? (*That's right!*)

Here's why: When other salespeople take time for a coffee break during the day, make another

appointment for that time instead. You'll gain an hour a day or nearly one extra day in every week!

3   Decide your priorities.

What comes first on your to-do list? Then second? Then third? Don't pick out number eight or nine because they're easier to do. First things first. Then number two becomes number one.

4   Decide to . . . do it!

When you decide what you want to do, and decide what you'll give up to do it, and decide your priorities—none of them mean anything unless you make the last decision: to do it!

Well, yes, there is another way. Another oil baron, John Paul Getty, once gave his three secrets of his success:

1   I got up early.

2   I worked hard.

3   My father struck oil.

Give 'em something extra.

IN NEW ORLEANS, they call it "lagniappe" (say lan-yap). Most call it "added value."

Added value means the unexpected, unadvertised, un-asked for "extra." Something the customer never expected after she made the decision to buy.

Example: The deliveryman from the furniture store who brings a dozen roses to place on the just-delivered dining room table.

Example: The small gift we gave to everyone who shopped in our retail stores the week before Thanksgiving to show our "thanks."

Example: When a family came to Zaberer's restaurant, the waitress would learn the name of the young child with his parents. At the end of the meal she would say to the child, "Mr. Zaberer told me he was watching you, Jacob, during your dinner and was so impressed with how polite you are that he wants you to have a gift certificate for a free meal when you come back next time."

(Guess who would demand to come back to Zaberer's for his free meal . . . and would bring his parents along as paying customers?)

Give customers what they want.

CUSTOMERS DON'T WANT anything—they want everything. And you have to find a way to give it to them.

Here's what customers want:

- Customization of the products they buy— Do they want the computer with 4 GB of RAM, 8 GB, or 16 GB? Do they want to send a $30, $50, or $75 bouquet of flowers? Customers want the product *their* way.

- Low price or fabulous service—Consumers don't want to pay more to buy it from you than they can to buy it elsewhere (and they will check) *unless* you offer service or product features not available anywhere else.

- Fast shipment—Two to three days is becoming the new norm. Can you ship items fast and reliably? And can you afford to ship them for free? Amazon Prime has upped the ante on shipping for everyone.

In most cases, there are lots of other places to buy your products. Cover the basics first so your customers aren't tempted to buy from someone else.

Learn how people read.

THERE HAS BEEN a lot of research on how people read—what they look at on the page first, second, and never. Learn from the experts to write your website and printed copy better.

Pepe Laja, digital marketing expert and founder of ConversionXL, gives these tips for how people look at websites:

- People look at the top left first. Put what you want customers to see first right there.

- Bigger, boldface introductory paragraphs draw attention.

- Use high quality, large images.

- First impressions take seconds. People focus on your logo, navigation menu, search box, the site's main image, and social media links.

Think of your website's home page, like a billboard—bold words, big image, and a headline.

When you are sending a letter (yes, people still use snail mail—and it can be quite effective), listen to the advice of Seigfried Vogele, who was dean of the Institute of Direct Marketing in Munich, Germany. His theories on the sales pitch by letter were based on eye-camera research. Vogele's insights have been used by leading direct marketing professionals around the world. Among Vogele's most important findings:

- The eye looks at illustrations first, then big type, then smaller type.

- People first read what's in the upper right hand corner of a letter (the opposite of how they look at a web page).

- Nine of ten readers look at a PS before reading the body of the letter.

- A customer spends seven seconds scanning the envelope, turning it over and deciding whether or not to open it. Once open, a customer spends eleven seconds deciding if the mailer is worth reading.

- If the person's name is spelled incorrectly, the reader stops reading.

There's a science to the way people read, both online and in print. Make your pitch more effective by knowing it.

Involve your staff.

SHOW YOUR ASSOCIATES a "rough" of your advertisement *before* it is finalized. You'll be amazed at the response.

Here are some comments we received from our staff when we gave them advance copies of mailers or ads. "You put in the wrong date" ... "The markdown isn't big enough to make anyone want to come". . . "I've spotted four misspellings so far" ... "You forgot to put in the name of our store."

The same rule works for your Internet site. Encourage all of your employees to test your website before it goes live. That's the quickest way to find broken links and places where the customer needs more information.

An added benefit: By involving your employees, you help them achieve satisfaction from their jobs. When he was a professor at Ohio State University, Ken Blanchard (of *The One Minute Manager* fame) did a comprehensive survey on what workers want from their jobs. "Being appreciated" was first and "being in on things" was second. "Higher wages" came in fifth.

There are only three ways to do more business.

HERE THEY ARE:

1 *Have more customers.* Makes sense. More customers = more dollars spent with you.

2 *Have customers shop more often.* If someone shops with you once a week, a month, or a year, and you can have her shop twice as often, you will double your business with that customer.

3 *Have customers buy more when they shop.* People shopping in a supermarket make 60 percent of their buying decisions while in the supermarket. They are attracted to end-aisle displays or walls of specials or sampling of new products. Think of the add-ons available to what-you-sell.

Offer a best-selling item on sale.

TOO MANY BUSINESSES think having a sale means offering huge markdowns on merchandise hasn't sold. Won't work. If it doesn't sell at regular price, you will sell very few on sale. Instead: offer a best-selling item on sale.

When customers come to buy this highly desired item, they'll also often buy other sale items you want them to buy.

Here's why: Having the customers open their wallets to buy the first item is the difficult task. Once they make the decision to buy something, they are then ready to buy additional items as well. Give them a reason to make that first purchase.

The second, third, and subsequent purchases will follow much easier.

Don't use percentages.

PEOPLE UNDERSTAND NUMBERS, but not percentages. They know what they are, but not what they mean.

The state of Florida gave a test to 130,000 high school juniors. One question referred to an ad for jeans:

"Regularly $60, now 20 percent off." The question asked: "How much would you save on two pairs?" (Answer: $24)

High school juniors with ten years of schooling could not figure the answer.

Conclusion: Do the math for the reader. If you say "30 percent off," *also* tell the original and the sale price.

Another tip: Your customers will understand "half price" better than "50 percent off."

WARNING: Do *not* use the words "up to" as in "up to 40 percent off." The customer immediately thinks almost everything is 10 percent off—or lower.

Ideate.

I'VE OFTEN BEEN asked, "How do you come up with new ideas that will work?"

I use these five steps written in the 1930s by James Webb Young, a member of the Advertising Hall of Fame.

1   Gather the material. Learn all you can about the product you want to sell. Write it down.

2   Think about it. Have a mental brainstorming session with yourself. Write down all your ideas, no matter how far-reaching or implausible.

3   Forget about the problem. Even though you dismiss the problem, your subconscious mind

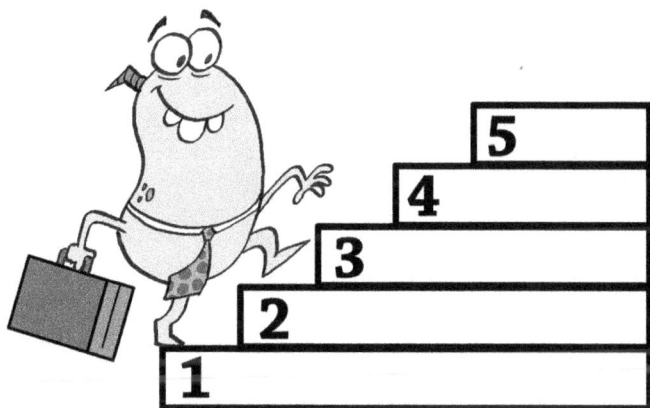

is still working on it.

4 The solution appears! When least expected. The idea will suddenly emerge, unannounced.

5 Do it. Then share your idea with other salespeople and you'll find they will say phrases like, "That makes a lot of sense—I have a couple of thoughts to make it a little better."

Everybody sells.

"We are all salespeople."
— *J. C. Penney*

TY BOYD, A motivational speaker and trainer, begins many of his programs by asking his audience, "Let me see the hands of all the salespeople in the audience."

About one-third of the people in the audience raise their hands.

Ty looks around the room and then asks, "What do the rest of you do for a living?"

His point: Everybody sells.

It is important that everyone who works for

your company understands that one of the primary purposes of a business is to make money (some commentators even opine that it is the "sole" purpose of a business). In order to make money, everybody involved in a business should focus on selling—the customer transaction that enables a business to make money.

Marketing consultant Alan Gold says, "In any successful company, everyone sells, from the clerk in the mailroom to the executives in the boardroom."

If you don't motivate your frontline people to be salespeople, you are missing a great opportunity. Tom Haggai, former CEO of IGA Supermarkets, said that a store's most important customers are its cashiers. The cashiers interact with customers all day long. If the cashiers are happy, they'll be selling to customers all day long, with favorable opinions about the store and the store's products.

But if cashiers are unhappy, customers will certainly notice and will leave the supermarket with negative feelings.

Enjoy your work.

THERE CAN BE no more horrible punishment than waking in the morning and dreading going to work. It's a shame if your only positive thought about work is looking forward to retirement when "I can do what I always wanted to do."

I once did a seminar in Arizona for franchise holders of a printing company. During my speech I said, "If you don't like what you're doing, quit! Do something you want to do. Not liking your work means not succeeding. We only pass this way but once."

One person in the audience approached me afterwards and said, "I wake up every morning feeling sick. I hate doing what I do. Thanks for your

advice. I'm quitting tomorrow and doing something I want to do."

She wrote me a year later and told me how it was the best decision she ever made. And she told me about her new and successful art gallery.

As Steve Jobs said, "I have looked in the mirror every morning and asked myself: 'If today were the last day of my life, would I want to do what I am about to do today?' And whenever the answer has been 'No' for too many days in a row, I know I need to change something."

Perfume

Have integrity.

WHAT DO PEOPLE think of you?

Are you known as the salesperson who cares about the customer? The one who has established a reputation of honesty and for selling a quality product?

If so, hold on to your reputation tightly. Do not change who-you-are because of economic conditions, the weather, or the time of the year.

I like how American Express handles complaints. It immediately credits the disputed amount back into its customer's account while it investigates the problem. Other companies treat customer complaints with suspicion and annoyance. American Express makes you think it is on your side.

Stanley Marcus, chairman of retailer Neiman-Marcus, explained this philosophy in his autobiography, *Minding the Store*. He said, "My father, burdened with a larger store and a backbreaking personal bank loan, stood firm and exhorted his buyers not to succumb to the temptation of cheaper inferior goods just to get badly needed sales. He urged them, time and again, to maintain the standards of quality our customers learned to expect from us."

Stanley Marcus and his father were models of integrity. No wonder they were able to help turn Neiman-Marcus into one of the most successful department stores in the country.

Be known for something that's yours alone.

WHEN WE FIRST started our children's clothing store, we looked for something that set us apart from similar stores in our city.

Our money for inventory was scarce. What could we offer that was inexpensive yet made us different?

We decided to buy large quantities of children's winter gloves, mittens, and hats. They were inexpensive to stock and we were able to advertise "The Largest Selection of Children's Winter Gloves, Mittens, and Hats."

People came to buy these items. And many also bought the more expensive snowsuits and coats.

When Ben Sears retired from the circus, he opened a small restaurant in San Francisco. How could he make his restaurant different?

Ben remembered his favorite meal to start the day: Swedish pancakes. The recipe was handed down through the generations of his wife Hilbur's Swedish family.

He offered 18 small pancakes for breakfast at a low price. They were an instant success.

Today, Sears Fine Food has people standing outside as early at 6:00 a.m. waiting for the store to open so they can order the "world famous Swedish pancakes." Sears makes 11,000 pancakes a day and sells the pancake mix to customers around the world.

Find a way to differentiate yourself from all your competitors. It can something small—ask Ben Sears!

RULE
43

Don't forget or change
what made you successful.

THE MUSEUM OF New Products had over 75,000 products that were testimony to the word "failure." Many came from successful brands.

Do you remember Coca-Cola clothes? They were made by Murjani and failed their second year.

Do you remember Bic perfume? Bic aftershave? Life Savers gum? Failed. Failed. Failed.

Pepsi Cola introduced clear Crystal Pepsi, and the consumer wondered, how could it be clear if it was cola? Clear was 7-Up. So what did 7-Up do? It introduced a cola-colored product called 7-Up Gold. And the consumer asked, how could it be 7-Up if it was cola-colored? Wasn't this the same company that

Pizzacycle

gained market share saying it was the Uncola? They lost $70 million on that one.

Once your brand is identified in the consumer's mind with one product, using that brand for a very different product confuses people and, even worse, results in losing sales of the original product.

Howard Schultz, CEO of Starbucks, summarizes the customer's relationship with a product's brand. "Great companies that build an enduring brand have an emotional relationship with customers that has no barrier. And that emotional relationship is on the most important characteristic, which is trust."

Study successful salespeople.

AN ISSUE OF *Forbes* magazine ran a story on one of America's top salesmen—Sid Friedman.

Sid had an insurance company, Corporate Financial Services, in Philadelphia, Pennsylvania, with more than 200 employees. He earned nearly three million dollars in personal commissions every year.

The top one-tenth of one percent of insurance salesmen belongs to an insurance group called "Top of the Table." Sid served as president. One of the most successful salespeople of his time, I offer a few of his sales ideas:

- "Every week call 100 people. Get 15 appointments. Sell three. Earn lots of money."

- "Some people work 52 weeks a year. I work 62 weeks a year. I come in one hour earlier than everyone else. I stay an extra hour later at night. Two hours a day. Five days a week. Ten hours a week. Gives me ten extra weeks."

- "Always give 100 percent! A satisfaction rate of 99.9 percent results in two unsafe plane landings at Chicago's O'Hare every day, 16,000 pieces of mail lost every hour, and 500 incorrect surgical performances every week."

- "Break rules. Discover what the rest of the world is doing and don't do it. Stop competing. Start creating. Have the courage to be different."

- "My philosophy is just ten words. Each has only two letters. Memorize them. Then do them. Here they are: 'If it is to be, it is up to me.'"

Sell one customer at a time.

I JUST FINISHED doing an all-day seminar for a hockey league franchise team.

The owner said, "I've been listening to you speak about marketing all day but you haven't given me the answer to the most important question."

"What's that?" I asked.

"My arena holds 10,000 people. How do I sell 10,000 tickets?"

I said, "One at a time."

"What's that mean?" he asked.

If you think in terms of big numbers you lose sight of how to get the big numbers.

The mind focuses better on small units. If 10,000

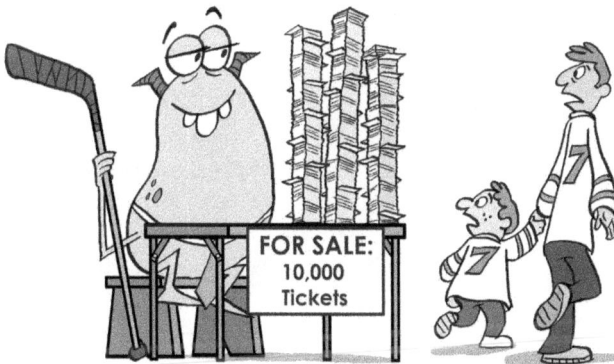

FOR SALE:
10,000
Tickets

people die in an earthquake in Bangladesh we are sympathetic but not involved.

But if we see pictures of a family of four who perished in a fire, our emotions are strong. We identify with the victims. You can see four people. You can't "see" 10,000 people who died in an earthquake halfway around the world.

We told the hockey club owner to spread the word about his team to people who influence lots of others. We said to start contacting leaders of local service clubs, concierges at the hotels, the head of the area convention center.

A journey to a faraway place begins with one step.

Compete with the giants with better service.

"The bigger the world economy, the more powerful its smaller players."
—*John Naisbitt, Global Paradox*

THE TOP TEN retailers in the US do 20 percent of the nation's business, close to a trillion dollars a year.

Question: How does the small retailer compete?

Answer: With service.

Service is a small retailer's greatest weapon. The average retail business trains new salespeople less than ten hours, according to the *New York Times*. For most of America's businesses the term "customer service" is an oxymoron.

My friend Ken Erdman and his wife were shopping in a major department store.

His wife selected several items but couldn't find anyone to ring up the sale. Ken walked to the middle of the store and, in a loud voice, yelled, "Help! Help! Help!" He was immediately surrounded by several security people who asked him his problem.

"No problem," said Ken, "I just want someone to *help* me."

So the next time you are challenged to play the competitive game of Winners and Losers, remember that the philosophy of many of the big guys is this: the customer is *anyone and everyone*. Your philosophy is the customer is *someone*. By treating customers the way you want to be treated, you increase your company's ability to compete effectively against much bigger entities.

Author Tony Allesandra says, "Being on par in terms of price and quality only gets you into the game. Service wins the game."

Have an invisible cabinet.

WHENEVER I HAVE a selling problem I cannot solve, I gather the members of my "invisible cabinet" to ask their advice.

My cabinet is made up of the best salespeople I have met, known, or read about. They are "invisible" because their existence is make-believe, but they are very helpful when a selling problem presents itself.

I know from their writings and philosophy what they would probably do in a given circumstance.

When I have a problem thinking of an advertising campaign, I turn to David Ogilvy, one of the best headline and copywriters of all time. Ben Feldman, one of the top life insurance salesmen ever, is always around to help me solve a sales problem.

None of your problems are really new. They existed for other salespeople sometime, somewhere. How did *they* handle a similar problem?

I mentally go around the room asking each for their advice and help. From their personal experience and knowledge, each will come up with an answer.

When a difficult situation arises it really helps to have the wisdom of others you trust and admire to help you arrive at a solution—even when they're invisible.

Practice the Rule of Three.

"The rule of three doth puzzle me."
—*John Napier, 1570*

THERE IS A rhythm in selling that works when
you plan, write, and create in threes.

Remember the number of Old King Cole's
fiddlers, the men in a tub, the total of blind mice,
and how much wool the black sheep had?

A young woman uses the rule in terms of potential dates (Tom, Dick, and Harry) and what
they'll look like (tall, dark, and handsome) but
she has to keep in mind that three is a crowd.

We start our school day saluting the flag with its colors of red, white, and blue, first learn the three primary colors, start our education with reading, 'riting, and 'rithmetic.

All successful selling plans have a beginning, middle, and end. What do you want to sell? What is your plan to sell it? What is your final argument to sell it?

Robert O. Skovgard, editor of *The Executive Speaker* newsletter said, "The most powerful and versatile speech writing devices or techniques involve grouping of elements in units of three." He gave some examples:

"Of the people, by the people, and for the people."
—*Abraham Lincoln*

"Duty, honor, country"
—*Douglas MacArthur*

"Liberty and union, now and forever, one and inseparable."
—*Daniel Webster*

When preparing for your next sale, remember the rule of three. List three benefits, three reasons to buy, and three ways to purchase.

Your sales will increase—perhaps as much as threefold!

Fear of loss is far more powerful than promise of gain.

TELLING THE CUSTOMER what he will gain from what you are selling is a strong selling technique.

More powerful: telling him what he will *lose* if he does not buy.

The Franklin Mint offered the first of a series of limited edition collector's plates. It advertised only a limited amount available. After that there would be no more. The die cast aside. The edition never made again.

Many customers ordered late.

They were shocked to have their checks returned with the note, "Sorry, the edition is sold out."

What happened the next time the Franklin Mint offered a limited edition? Yes! It was sold out almost immediately.

No one wanted to lose the opportunity to buy.

When preparing your selling presentation, think about what the customer will lose if he does not buy.

When you speak first, you lose.

WHEN YOU HAVE made your presentation, stop!

Don't add anything. Don't break the silence. Because the tension grows with each passing moment. Someone has to say something. If the customer speaks first, you have an immediate idea of her concern and can answer any question.

Most salespeople can't stand this pressure of silence and quickly offer another advantage, a reduction in price, another reason for buying.

Stop! Listen.

This rule works for us in hotels where the clerk

says, "Sorry, there are no more rooms." There's always a room somewhere. But not if you break the silence and say, "Well, okay, thanks anyway."

Just stand there. Say nothing, and more often than not, a room will become available. A reservation at the restaurant can be gotten, perhaps at a different time than you requested—but available. An appointment with a doctor or dentist where you are squeezed in after being told, "the doctor's hours are filled."

Make the request. Say what you want.

Then say nothing.

Be prepared.

DALE CARNEGIE TOLD the story of Wallace Donham, dean of the Harvard Business School, who said, "I should rather walk the sidewalk in front of a man's office for two hours before an interview than step into his office without a perfectly clear idea of what I'm going to say and what he—from my knowledge of his interest and motive—is likely to answer."

The customer knows why you want him to buy. You take his money and put it in your pocket.

But what's in it for him?

Aristotle said all persuasion comes from one of

three sources: Facts and logic. Emotional appeals. And the confidence the listener has in the person speaking. A top salesperson needs to use all three of these resources.

Preparation. It's the Boy Scout motto.

It's also the salesperson's motto.

Don't close the sale.

I'D BE THE first to agree that a goal of selling is to get the order.

But why does it have to depend on "the close?"

The first definition of "closing" in Webster's is "to bar passage."

The second definition says, "to deny access to."

The third definition is "to suspend or stop operations."

The fourth definition: "to bring to an end."

A closing thus defeats your primary goal in selling: the lifetime value of the customer.

You don't "close" the sale. You "open" relationships. Isn't the end of the first sale really the beginning of the *next* sale to the same customer? (Answer: Yes.)

It is no longer enough to make the sale. It's important, but not enough.

It is no longer enough to follow through. It's important, but not enough.

It is no longer enough to remind the customer you're still doing business at the same stand with new and improved products. It's important, but not enough.

It is no longer enough to sell the product and the values that surround the purchase. It's important, but not enough.

It is all of these. And more.

There is no close.

There is only a beginning.

PS: Check up on yourself.

IT WAS SUMMERTIME. Our store was packed with shoppers. I was called from my office to help at the counter. A young man named Tommy came up to me and asked, "Mr. Raphel, can I use your phone?"

"Sure, Tommy," I said. After all, I knew Tommy all his life. I delivered his baby clothes to the hospital when he was born. He picked up the phone, dialed, and I heard him say, "Hi. I just went past your house. Saw you had a big lawn. I cut lawns to make some extra money. I also trim hedges. And I was wondering if . . ."

He paused, listened, then continued, "I see. Are you satisfied with the work they're doing?"

Another pause.

"I see. Well, would it be all right if I called you

back in a month or so to see if you're still satisfied? I can? Thank you."

And hung up.

I walked over to him and said, "Tommy, forgive me. But I was standing here and heard your conversation. I want you to know that everything you said was right. Promise me you won't be disappointed because you didn't get the sale."

"Oh, Mr. Raphel," he said, "I got the sale. That was one of my customers. I was just checking up to see how I'm doing."

YOU GOTTA KNOW THE
Rules!